Carpe Diem

Ekta

BookLeaf Publishing
India | USA | UK

Presentation by *BookLeaf Publishing*

Web: www.bookleafpub.com

E-mail: info@bookleafpub.com

ISBN: 9789360942632

First edition 2024

Tell me Goodbye.....

The memories of you
are engraved within my heart
Nothing in this world
Could ever tear us apart.

I try to stay positive,
to keep you watching over me
People may think it's crazy
But I know you've got to be.

I spend most of my time
thinking of you
And reminiscing of the things
We thought we would do.

What I wouldn't give
to be in your place?
I'd give the whole world
Just to see your face.

Am I going crazy
Or maybe insane
I fail to understand,
this heartbreaking pain.

I've been thinking of the day
all the times that we spent together
I now cherish those moments
I also hope you remember.

You're always in my head,
And I can't get you out
I get so mad at times
That I just want to shout.

I feel as if pieces are missing
Like a book with no end
Too late to tell you how I feel,
Now and forever, only a friend?

All the sweet thoughts of you
Bring a tear to my eye
I miss you so much
I wish you'd said goodbye....

I hope heaven's good to you
And I hope you get your wings

And maybe when I get there
You can show me all the beautiful things.

I really don't want to say it
But please wait for me.
Knowing you're up there,
I really can’t wait to be.
That day when Angels came down
Was a sad day of grief.
When I first found out,
I stood in disbelief.

Although you are gone
You still feel so close
Maybe it's the thought,
of missing you the most.

I wish this was a joke
a stupid little lie
But you've no idea
Please.... tell me goodbye...

The Friend I needed the most

In the depths of my despair, you appeared
A beacon of light in my darkest hour
Your presence like a gentle breeze
Soothing my battered soul, bringing me peace

Thank you for being the friend I needed the most
In times of joy and times of sorrow
You stand by my side, unwavering and true
A pillar of strength, a guiding light

Through laughter and tears, you've been my rock
Listening without judgment, understanding without words
Your kindness and compassion know no bounds
In you, I've found a friend for life

Thank you for being the friend I needed the most
For lifting me up when I was down
For believing in me when I couldn't see
For being the anchor in my stormy sea

I cherish our bond, our shared moments
Each memory a treasure, each laugh a gift
I am grateful for your friendship, your love
Thank you for being the friend I needed the most

Being a Potterhead- For you, Daiwik

Oh, the magic that flows through my veins,
As a Potterhead, I'm never in pain.
The wizarding world, it calls to me,
A place where I can be free.

The wand chooses the wizard, they say,
But I know I've chosen the wand's way.
With a flick of my wrist, I can cast a spell,
And make the impossible, possible as well.

The adventures I've had, the memories I've made,
All because of the Boy Who Lived, the one they called brave.

Harry Potter, the Chosen One,
His story is the one that's won.

The Hogwarts Express, it takes me away,
To a place where magic is forever to stay.
The Forbidden Forest, it's my home,
Where I can be myself, and never feel alone.

The spells I've learned, the potions I've brewed,
The wonders I've seen, the dreams I've pursued.
I'm a Gryffindor, through and through,
Forever a Potterhead, that's what I'll do.

So let the magic flow, let it fill my heart,
For being a Potterhead, is a work of art.

Paris, always my first love

In Paris, the city of love and light,
Where the Seine River dances with delight,
I found my heart's first love, so pure and bright,
In the City of Love, my heart took flight.

The Eiffel Tower stands tall and proud,
A symbol of love that will never cloud,
The Louvre's art and beauty astound,
In Paris, my heart was forever bound.

The streets of Montmartre, so charming and quaint,
Where artists once plied their trade and gained,
The scent of freshly baked croissants, baguette and pain,
In Paris, my love for life was regained.

The bridge of Pont des Arts, a work of art,
Where lovers stroll and play their part,

The Luxembourg Gardens, a gem so rare,
In Paris, my heart found its lair.

The city's magic, a spell so strong,
That keeps me coming back, all day long,
In Paris, my first love will always be,
The city of love, a dream for me!

A little peace and quiet

Where my heart truly lies
Is in the beauty of a simple life,
In a little peace and quiet,
Slower pace and lesser strife.

Where I'd find time to walk
Leisurely down a winding road,
Strolling in the woods, savoring
Each unfolding scenic episode.

Where I'd find time to sit
And nestle by the almond tree,
Feeling its quiet windy whispers
As it gently cuddles me.

Where I'd find time to stand
Quietly behind the windowpane,

Cradling a mug, watching the world
Showered with a gentle rain.

Where I'd find time to catch
The sparkling poise of a firefly
And lounge in the serene canopy
Of a star-speckled velvet sky.

Just a little peace and quiet,
In between life's hectic pace...
And I find my soul better aligned,
Filled with sweet solace.

I long for the ocean breeze
To feel the wind upon my skin
Like a thousand soft kisses,
Its finger through my hair
Like a passionate lover!!!

A Birthday, so special

This birthday, a celebration like never before
A symphony of emotions, a chorus of joy
Surrounded by love, enveloped in warmth
A birthday like never before, a treasure full of memories

The candles flicker, casting a soft glow
Dancing shadows on the walls, a ballet of light
Laughter echoes in the room, music to my ears
Each moment a precious gift, each smile a work of art

Friends and family gather, a tapestry of faces
Each thread woven with care, each connection a bond
Hugs and kisses shared, a language of love

A birthday like never before, a masterpiece in
the making

The clock ticks on, the night grows late
But time stands still in this moment of bliss
For in this space, in this place
I am surrounded by love, by warmth, by magic

A birthday like never before, a new chapter in
the book of life
A story to be told, a memory to be cherished
And as the day fades into night
I am grateful for this gift, this birthday like
never before!!!

You will live forever in my heart

In the quiet chambers of my soul,
Where memories linger like echoes,
You will live forever in my heart,
A flame that never flickers or fades.

Your laughter dances in the shadows,
A melody that plays on repeat,
And I find solace in the thought,
That you are never truly gone.

In the stillness of the night,
I feel your presence, warm and bright,
A guiding light in times of darkness,
A flare of love that never wanes.

Though time may pass and seasons change,
The imprint of your spirit remains,
Etched deep within my very being,
A timeless bond that can't be broken.

So rest in peace, dear one,
For in my heart, you'll always stay,
A cherished memory, a sacred vow,
You will live forever in my heart!

Who am I?

Who am I, in this vast and complex world?
A mere mortal, with a story yet to unfold
A speck of dust, floating in the grand scheme
A puzzle piece, searching for its team

Am I defined by my name or my appearance?
Or the roles I play in this earthly interference?
Am I just a product of my past and present?
Or do I have a destiny, yet to be evident?

I am a collection of memories and dreams
A canvas, painted with hopes and schemes
I am a melody, with lyrics untold
A book, with chapters yet to unfold

I am the sum of my triumphs and falls
The scars and bruises, that adorn my walls
I am the laughter, that echoes in the night
And the tears, that fall in the absence of light

I am a student, learning from life's lessons
A wanderer, in search of hidden blessings
I am a warrior, fighting my own battles
A survivor, of life's unpredictable rattles

I am a reflection of those I hold dear
The love and support, that I hold near
I am a part of something greater than me
A thread, in the fabric of humanity

Who am I, you may ask once again
I am a human, with flaws and strengths within
A soul, on a journey of self-discovery
And every day, I am becoming a better version
of me.

A poem in the making

A poem in the making
A journey of words and rhymes
A canvas for my thoughts
A melody in time

It starts with a spark
A flicker in my mind
A feeling that ignites
A story to unwind

I pick up my pen
And let the ink flow
As the words dance on paper
A story starts to grow

Each line a reflection
Of my heart and soul
A glimpse into my world
A map to my goal

With every stanza
A piece of me is revealed
A poem in the making
A truth that's unsealed

The rhythm takes over
As I lose myself in the flow
The words become my guide
As my emotions start to show

It's a journey of discovery
As I explore my deepest fears
A poem in the making
A release of all my tears

And when the final verse is written
And the last word is said
A poem in the making
Is a masterpiece instead

For it's not just words on paper
But a piece of my heart
A poem in the making
A reflection of my art!

Dreams

Images of hope,
Locked up fear you share,
Love and desire,
All in your head somewhere.

Dreams are wishes
That let your imagination grow.
They let you travel
Anywhere you can go.

Dreams show your happiest moments,
And what you dread in your heart.
They show you love, how to hold it,
And tell you where to start.

You could feel the beach,
The sand at your feet,
The heart and soul you'll be able to reach.

Words and images swirl in your mind
That let you express yourself all the time.

And when horrors are received,
And I fall on my knees,
Everything is softened by the memories, the dreams.

This is how you fall out of love

This is how you fall out of love:
Slowly, like the setting sun
Each day brings a little less warmth
A little less light

It starts with a glance
A moment of hesitation
A doubt that creeps in
And slowly takes hold

You start to notice the little things
The way they chew their food
The way they breathe in their sleep
The way they never listen

You find yourself picking fights
Searching for an excuse to leave
To break free from the ties that bind
From the love that once felt so right

You start to drift apart
Like ships passing in the night
No longer connected
No longer in sync
You stop holding hands
Stop saying "I love you"
Stop looking into each other's eyes
And start looking away

The love that once burned so bright
Fades into a distant memory
A ghost of what once was
A shadow of what could have been

And then one day, you wake up
And realize that you're not in love anymore
That the fire has died out
That what once seemed so perfect
Is now just a shell of its former self

And so you walk away
With a heavy heart
With a sense of loss
But also a sense of relief

Because this is how you fall out of love
Slowly, quietly, painfully
Until one day, you realize
That it's time to let go....

Inner Peace

The wind whistles past my ears.
Closing my eyes, I lose all my fears.
The waves crash into the rocks.
Out here there is no time on my clock.

The serenity I feel here just soothes my mind.
A peaceful day so hard to find.
The breeze just calms my soul.
Helps me think about what is my life's goal.

I then look out over the ocean,
And it feels like my life has lost its commotion.
The sun sets down over the clouds.
But the orange glow around makes me proud.

As the night draws near.
I feel like where I need to be is here.
The soothing nature this afternoon brings
Just feels like such a beautiful thing.

I sit and wonder where life will go,
But right now all I want is for time to slow.
To enjoy this moment and feel free,
To clear my mind and find some glee.

It's days like these I truly treasure.
Amazing nights and beautiful weather.
It may not seem like much.
But it's moments like these I want to clutch.

For once I feel like life is bliss.
So many hard days in which my happiness was
missed.
I could get lost listening to the waves.
Listening to the birds and watching how the
clouds behave.

I could close my eyes and fade into the night.
The tranquility I feel helps me win the fight.
As the waves keep crashing into the rocks,
I feel the happiness in my heart become
unlocked.

The day is drawing to a close.
The peacefulness I feel right now I'll only know.
Right now my mind is finally clear.
It's time to go as the night draws near.

A Teacher by day, a Poet by night

In the light of day, she stands tall and strong
Guiding eager minds, shaping the future
With patience and wisdom, she imparts her knowledge
A ray of hope in a world of uncertainty

But when the sun dips below the horizon
And shadows dance across the page
She becomes a wordsmith, a creator of beauty
A poet weaving dreams with ink and imagination

Her classroom transforms into a canvas
Where words paint pictures of love and loss
Of hope and despair, of joy and sorrow
Each line a brushstroke, each stanza a masterpiece

The moonlight whispers secrets in her ear
Inspiring verses that flow like a river
Her heart spills out onto the page
A teacher by day, a poet by night

For in her words, she finds solace
A refuge from the chaos of the world
And in the silence of the night
She finds her true voice, her true self

So let her be both teacher and poet
Let her light shine bright in the darkness
For in her hands, lies the power of words
To heal, to inspire, to change the world.

Being a teenager's mom

Being a teenager's mom,
Is like riding a rollercoaster,
Full of ups and downs,
And unexpected twists and turns.

One moment he is happy and carefree,
The next he is moody and withdrawn,
But through it all, I must stay strong,
And guide him as he grows.

It's a constant battle of wills,
As he tries to assert his independence,
But I must balance discipline and love,
And teach him right from wrong.

I watch him spread his wings,
And soar into the world,
But my heart aches with worry,
As I hope he will make the right choices.

I am his confidant and his friend,
But also his protector and his guide,
As he navigates through the challenges,
Of being a teenager in this crazy world.

I witness his first heartbreak,
And hold him as he cries,
I celebrate his achievements,
And encourage him to reach for the sky.

Being a teenager's mom,
Is a journey like no other,
But I wouldn't trade it for anything,
For he is my heart and soul.

And though there may be days,
When I feel like I'm losing control,
I know deep down in my heart,
That being his mom is my greatest role.

So I'll cherish every moment,
Of this wild and crazy ride,
For being a teenager's mom,
Is a blessing I'll forever hold with pride.

Whispering Waves

Waves come crashing to grey sullen shores.
Powerful and strong, it breathes and roars.
Cascading and caressing each grain of sand,
A warm embrace between sea and land.

High above, a seagull soars high.
Wings of purity it spreads to fly.
Battling high against darkened cloud,
In a wind that blows fiercely, flying graceful and proud.

Beneath, the sand is soft and warm.
Sculpted by nature, it weathered the storm.
A passionate battle between calmness and rage,
A new chapter's beginning; don't turn the last page.

I listen again to the whispering waves,
Music of nature, calming and brave.
Its power unknown, its stillness untamed,
Mysterious and magical, a treasure earth claims.

Through the eyes of a child

I have climbed the highest mountain
And sailed the ocean wide
But nothing could ever fill my heart
Like a smile from a child

I have seen the sunsets
That would take your breath away
But nothing could ever shine so bright
When a child is brought our way

When temptations were so many
And I dealt with selfish pride
Nothing could ever turn my head
Like a cry from a child

This life is filled with obstacles
That makes us want to hide
But the world will always turn on time
Through the eyes of a child

I have seen my days of sadness
And worry was so much
And nothing could ever clear my mind
Like a child's gentle touch

And I have walked through darkened valleys
And travelled wayward miles
But nothing could stop me in my tracks
Like a smile from a child

Our lives are set on a time scale
The clock will tick away
But there are no minutes for us to count
When a child has asked to play

These eyes of mine are growing old
The future I cannot see
But the world never felt so much at peace
When a child sits on my knees

I have lived my life on chance
And that's how it was meant to be
But I've always had an angel
To watch carefully over me

God send us guardian angels
And we know not what their size
To help us with this life down here
To walk us through our miles

God send you this blessing
A little angel comes your way
To fill your heart with happiness
With every passing day
So lift your arms to heaven
And hold them open wide
God send you a life of treasures
Through the eyes of a child!

Life is all you make of it

How do we measure success in this life?
And who should decide if you fail?
Do life's sweet temptations guide you along?
Or in the end does your conscience prevail?

Is life just a game that you play everyday?
Bending the rules for yourself,
Desperately chasing material goals,
To the ruin of everything else.

Do you cherish the people around you?
Or do you squander the love that they share?
Do you take time to notice the efforts they make?
Or do you treat them as if they aren't there?

Do you wake up each morning just to be grateful,
Thanking God when you open your eyes!
And how many dawns do you gaze at the sky?
And stop to behold the sunrise?

How many moments in the course of your day,
Do you treasure each second of time?
Embracing the sad and the sweet that is there,
With the whole of your heart, soul and mind.

And despite any anger you suffer inside,
From the hurt and betrayals of life,
Do you manage to keep your own self-respect?
Or are you led by your own foolish pride?

Do you live by the motto forgive and forget?
Or are you consumed by the need for revenge?
Do you try every day to live open in truth?
Or is your life just a game of pretense?

For those who are young and new to this world,
So filled with hopes and dreams,
Take my advice, don't complicate life,
It is simpler than sometimes it seems.

For when you have reached the twilight of life,
All the answers are finally revealed,
And that search and struggle that left you
confused,
With hindsight it becomes crystal clear.

Hold fast to that childhood passion and awe,
Cling to each moment you get,

Let your heart feel completely each feeling you have,
And give the people you love, all your best.

Don’t waste or misuse this wonderful gift,
Don’t surrender or grow too complacent,
Remember in the end it’s all up to you,
And life can be all that you make of it!

A reason to survive

Sometimes you have to push yourself just to get out of bed
You stay up until 2am just wishing you were dead
You ask yourself, "Why can't it be someone else instead?"
You get tired of all the thoughts in your head.

You lose sight of who you want to be
You blame yourself, screaming, "Why am I me?"
You wish you could just be free
Open your eyes and you'll see.

That life is what you make it, and sometimes it's hard
We get battered and bruised, mistreated and scarred.

We forget what's important
We forget our drive
We all need a focus point
A reason to survive.

Find your passion
Find your drive
Find something that makes you fight
And you will survive!!!

While walking on the beach……

You look out into the water;
The waves make the most beautiful sound.
A place you find peace and comfort,
Walking hand in hand and looking around.

As you walk towards the water,
Sand coats the bottom of your feet.
The smell of the sea salt draws you closer,
The view is so beautiful, oh so sweet.

Almost as if it is calling you.
Sometimes it's only in your mind.
A place to clear your thoughts
And leave everything very far behind.

You find shells, rocks, and other things.
The warmth is like a kiss from up above.
Looking out into the coast
Can only remind you of true love.

As the waves come crashing in,
Time seems to be standing still.
The sun is shining down on you
As you walk the beach at your will.
Paradise you thought you could never reach.
Out in the distance you can see the ships sailing by.
Tears of joy for the scene God has put before you,
As the moment makes you cry.

Two shadows are together as one,
A sign of great unity.
A great day full of fun
While walking on the beach....

The language of your heart

Each day we wake is such a gift,
No moments guaranteed.
Tomorrow isn't promised,
But to fate we must concede.

We cannot know our futures,
How long or short are our lives.
We simply do the best we can,
Until the end arrives.

And in life, what's most important,
In the scheme of everyday,
Are the people who stand by our sides,
As we venture on our way.

Those cherished, loyal, patient souls,
Who take us as we are,
Who look beyond our foolishness,
Our frailties and our scars.

How often do we take the time,
To lay our hearts down bare,
And tell them how we truly feel,
And just how much do we care?

Do we freely give a compliment,
And acknowledge efforts made?
Or do our own quite fragile egos
Make us feel far too afraid?

Have we tried to overcome our pride,
And forgive another's wrongs?
Or do we cling to hurt and anger,
And carry grudges far too long?

Do we share our blessings willingly,
With those who are in need?
Or do we hoard our own good fortune,
Out of selfishness and greed?

It's the people all around us,
Who makes us who we are.
It is they who save our erring souls
And fill our lovely hearts.

So it's time we show some gratitude,
And not wait for another day.
For before we even know it,
Our chance may slip away.

It’s past time to say I love you,
And forgive another’s sins.
We must let ourselves be vulnerable,
By letting others in.
For one day, tomorrow will not come;
We may not meet again.
For inevitably, for each of us,
It all comes to an end.

So go ahead and say the words;
Make today a start,
Don’t regret your silence;
Share the language of your heart.

Summer break- a time to build new memories

In the hazy days of summer break
We gather together, hearts full and light
To build new memories, pure and bright
Under the warm sun's gentle wake
Free from the shackles of daily grind
We roam the world like carefree souls
Exploring lands, chasing dreams untold
On adventures of a most wondrous kind
The days stretch out before us, endless and free
Filled with laughter, joy, and simple pleasures
We watch the sunset paint the sky in treasures
And feel the peace of nature's soothing decree
We dip our toes in cool, refreshing streams
And dance in meadows of wildflowers sweet
Our spirits lifted by the rhythm of summer's beat
As we let go of stress and old self-esteem
In these fleeting moments of joy and bliss

We forge bonds that will stand the test of time
And weave stories that will forever shine
In our hearts, sealed with a kiss
So let us cherish this time of magic and wonder
Embrace the warmth that surrounds us all
And let our spirits rise, never to fall
In the embrace of summer break, ever so tender.

Heartbreak

In the quiet aftermath of shattered dreams,
I find myself adrift in a sea of heartbreak.
The pain is a fierce, relentless tide,
Dragging me down into its depths,
Leaving me gasping for air.
I thought we were forever,
Bound together by a love so pure,
But now I see the cracks in our foundation,
The flaws in our once perfect union.
I gave you my heart, my soul,
And you tossed them aside like they meant
nothing.
The memories of our time together
Haunt me like ghosts in the night,
Whispering of what we once had,
But can never have it again.

I try to hold on to the fragments of us,
But they slip through my fingers like sand,
Leaving me broken and alone.
I thought I knew what love was,
But now I realize I was naive,
Blinded by the intensity of my feelings.
Love is not always enough,
It cannot fix what is broken,
And sometimes it is better to let go,
Even though it feels like ripping out a piece of my soul.
So I stand here, in the wreckage of our love,
Trying to find a way to piece myself back together,
To mend the cracks in my heart.
But the scars you left behind will always remind me
Of the pain of heartbreak,
A pain that will never truly heal.

Do Dreams Come True?

When we first met, I was lost
Lost in the deep moonlight ocean
That I found in his eyes
When we first met, I was lost
Lost in the pale pink rose
That I found resting upon his cheek
When we first met, I was lost
Lost in the light brown bark of a tree
That I found on his skin
When we first met, I was lost
Lost in the pearls
That I found just underneath those perfect lips
When he left, I was lost
Lost in a whole new way
No more deep blue eyes
No more pink roses

No more perfect pearls
And when he left, I was lost
Lost in the sorrow
That I found in my heart
Night falls and morning comes and still no sign of you
I wonder what you're doing and wished I were there with you
I think about you every day
and hope you're missing me too

I know we'll be together someday 'cause dreams do come true.
But until we find each other all I can do
I dream of us together, alone, just me and you.

Through the Eyes of a Mother

Mother's first moment with the baby
In the hush of the hospital room,
where time stands still,
a mother's heart swells with love
as she holds her newborn child for the first time.
Tears of joy glisten in her eyes,
mirroring the innocence and purity
of the tiny being nestled in her arms.
Their souls intertwine in a dance of wonder,
a bond forged in the miracle of birth.
In this sacred moment of connection,
the world fades away
and all that exists is the love
between a mother and her baby.

She whispers words of love and promise,
vowing to protect and cherish,
to guide and nurture,
to be a beacon of light
in the darkness of the unknown.
And as she gazes into those trusting eyes,
she knows that she is forever changed,
transformed by the miracle of motherhood
and the boundless love that fills her heart.

Being a Single Mother

In a world where gender roles dictate,
The presence of a male is the mandate.
But why can't society see,
A family without him, can be complete and free?
A mother's love knows no bounds,
She can be both pillars, strong and sound.
She nurtures, protects, and guides,
Her child with unwavering pride.
Yet society fails to recognize,
That a family without a man can thrive.
For love knows no gender,
It's unconditional and tender.
A single mother's strength is unmatched,
She carries burdens far from detached.
Her love sustains her family whole,
Filling their hearts and souls.
So why must we adhere,
To outdated norms that instil fear?

A family is not defined by its structure,
But by the love that shines like a fixture.
So celebrate the strength of women
And the beauty of a family without limits or inhibition
For in their presence, one finds true peace
A family complete, love will never cease.

Is being gay an unnatural choice?

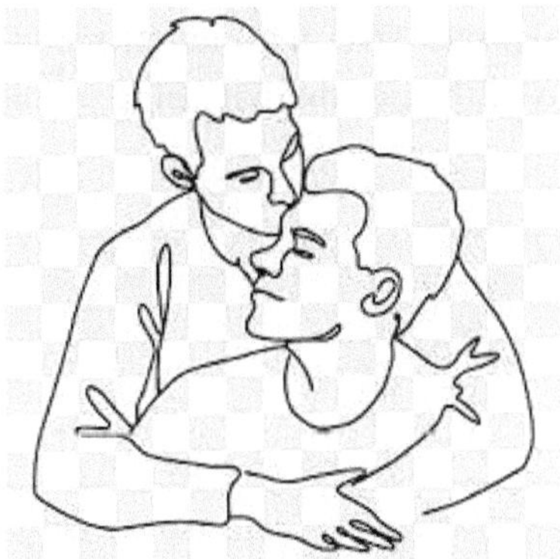

In a world that's constantly changing,
Where labels and judgments are always
rearranging,
There's a question that's often debated,
Is being gay a choice that's created?
Some say it's unnatural, goes against the norm,
But who decides what's right and what's wrong?
Is love not love, no matter the form?
Shouldn't we all be free to belong?
To love who we love, without fear or shame,
To live our truth, and not play a game,
Being gay is not a choice we make,
It's a part of who we are, not a mistake.
We are all born with love in our hearts,
No matter our gender, we all play a part,

So let's embrace diversity and understanding,
And let go of the hate and demanding.
Being gay is not a sin or a crime,
It's a beautiful part of the human design,
So let's celebrate love in all its forms,
And let go of the notion that being gay is the norm.

Sunset symphony

A canvas of colors painted in the sky,
As the sun bids farewell with a gentle sigh,
Golden hues melting into shades of red,
A symphony of emotions fills me instead.
The sky ablaze with fiery passion,
Embracing the darkness in a tender fashion,
The world bathed in a warm, radiant glow,
A kaleidoscope of feelings, ebb and flow.
The beauty of the moment, fleeting and
profound,
A silent orchestra without a single sound,
Emotions dance in the fading light,
As day turns into night, a magical sight.
The sun slowly sinking below the horizon,
Leaving behind a trail of memories to envision,
A bittersweet melody playing in the air,
As the sunset whispers of love and despair.
In this symphony of emotions, I find my peace,
As the colors fade and the darkness increase,

A reminder that endings are but beginnings in disguise,
And the sunset's beauty will forever mesmerise.
So I sit in awe of nature's grand display,
As the sun sets on another glorious day,
A symphony of emotions, a timeless refrain,
In the beauty of the sunset, I find solace again.

Take a moment

Take a moment.
Put the worries behind.
Take in the beauty around.
Let it relax your mind.
Watch the golden glow
Of the rising morning sun.
Embrace the peaceful aura
Of the break of dawn.
Savour the soft caress
Of the gently moving breeze.
Listen to its melodious tune
Among the swaying trees.
Enjoy the lovely scene
Of a floating butterfly.
Graceful flight and happy tweets
Of a bird perched up high.
Peruse the evening sky
In its dazzling splendor.
The wide and open pallet
Merging shapes and colors.
Relish the loving sight
Of children having fun,
Skipping feet and carefree voices
Under the setting sun.
Spare a still moment
Every once in a while.

Take in the beauty around.
Take it in with a smile.

Finding Me

I miss you in silence
And every moment in between
But I'm a little busy unfolding
These pieces of who I used to be
I miss you at sunrise
Until it's time to greet the moon
But darling,
Don't you see
I don't miss you any less than yesterday
I am just a little busy
Finding me!

A Woman

A woman is a wonder to behold,
A force of nature, strong and bold.
Her beauty shines both inside and out,
Her heart full of love and her mind devout.
Her eyes are pools of endless depth,
Reflecting the joys and pains she's kept.
Her voice can soothe, calm and inspire,
Lifting up those whose spirits tire.
Her hands are gentle, yet firm and sure,
Working hard with a heart so pure.
She brings forth life with each new birth,
Guiding her children through life's worth.
A woman's strength knows no bounds,
She overcomes, she perseveres, she astounds.
She is a warrior, a queen, a friend,
Her love and compassion knows no end.
So here's to the women of this world,
May your dreams and passions unfurl.

May you know your worth and never forget,
You are loved, respected, and a force to be
reckoned with.

We, the Women

We are soft and feminine,
Pretty and stylish,
We are strong in heart,
We keep going on and on,
We persevere...
Women are dependable,
Loving, and caring,
We keep our men going,
When times are rough,
We are very tough,
There are all kinds,
Of beautiful women,
In the world...
All shapes and sizes,
Different personalities,
We make up a good,

Part of the world,
We go through a lot,
We get the worst end,
Of breakups and heartache,
We get the emotional baggage,
The periods, the cramps,
But that is only,
A small fraction,
Of who we are,
We can be anyone we want!
We're independent,
We can be doctors,
Lawyers, teachers,
Journalists, surgeons,
Accountants, soldiers,
The world is our oyster,
And we are the pearls,
Love fills our souls,
We are so full of life,
We shine like diamonds,
In the night sky,
We may rise and fall,
But through it all,
We stand up tall.

That’s Me

“That’s Me”
Mature by mind but a kid by heart, rude from the outside but caring from the inside, egoistic
and full of attitude but also innocent and stupid.
Understand me. I am not like an ordinary world.
I have my madness, I live in another
dimension, and I do not have time for things that have no soul.
So don’t be too quick to judge!

Love will find its way

I always knew that love would come find me someday,
but never did I know that it would be you who was headed my way.
You caught me off guard and took me by surprise,
and you simply captivated me, the same way you would do when I looked into your eyes.
It's true that every good and perfect gift is from above.
You were presented to me as a beautifully packaged gift full of humor, talent, intelligence, and love.
"It isn't finding the perfect person but learning to see an imperfect person perfectly."

We all have our flaws, but when I see you
through my eyes, perfection is all I see.
From when you laugh to when you're quiet, I
still love the little things you do,
especially hearing you laugh and seeing your
face wrinkle the same way mine does too.
Coming into this relationship has been hard at
times, but we've made it through.
I know as long as we're on this journey together,
there's nothing that we can't do.
Sometimes I wonder if what we have is too good
to be true.
Too scared to get my heart broken and scared of
the thought of losing you,
but in the end, I trust in the Almighty that I
believe
because what we ask for in Him, we in return
shall receive.
"Where your treasure is, your heart will also be"
is how the saying goes.
I may not know what tomorrow may bring, for
God is the only one who knows.
The one thing I do know is that you are that one
and only,
a treasure in my heart that I would want to spend
my whole life with, completely.
I know I don't need to prove my feelings to
know they're true

because what I've known in my past doesn't
come close to the experience I've shared with
you.
I've had the experience of being in a relationship
before,
however, this is the first time I've been truly
happy... I couldn't ask for anything more.
It's an honor to know that I may be yours, as you
would be mine,
and I trust God that He'll bring us together in His
beautiful time.
For now, I'll be waiting patiently for that day
when we can be together,
that precious moment in time when I'll say, "It's
you that I want to be with forever."
God made everything beautiful, precious and
new,
just as beautiful and precious as the day will be,
when I look into your eyes and say, "I Love
You."

Love- A gift from God

Love can't be described.
It has no shape, it has no form.
Love is not an object.
Love does not conform.
Love enters our lives
The moment we are born.
From the cradle to the grave,
Love's in everyone.
Love burns like a candle
That sometimes flickers but never dies.
Love may be invisible,
Although it's right before your eyes,
Love can leave you empty,
Love can make you whole.
Love can make or break you,
Love is in your soul.
Love is in your heart,
Love is in your mind.

Love doesn't discriminate,
Love is always blind.
Love is universal,
It encompasses the globe.
No matter where you are,
Love has a language all its own.
Love is all around you.
There's plenty of love to spare.
You cannot see or touch it,
But love is everywhere.
Love's the greatest power,
And yet it is so small.
Love's a gift from God
To be shared amongst us all.

Have you ever had that moment?

Have you ever had that one moment?
That one moment,
Where you realize this is what you've been waiting for your whole life.
That what you have now is fate,
And knowing that makes your heart swell and your face light up.
You just feel as if everything in the world is right for once.
As if love is the only thing that exists.
No hatred. No lies. No betrayal.
When you've learned to fly.
And you take off to new heights,
And you never want to come back down.
Hope takes over your mind and you can never wipe that smile away.
That moment,
Where you finally realize love truly exists,
And you are a part of it now.
That moment,
Where you want to hold on to them and never let go.
That moment,
Where things fall into their rightful place.
Well, my moment is now.

Behind my smile….

Behind my smile lie my fears
Behind those laughs I hide my tears
I'm one of those you call fake
And the more I go the more I ache
I have a dark secret I cannot tell
Sometimes it feels like a wizard's spell
I've been told it's not my fault
How could I know it was assault?
I still see him everywhere
Why is that? It's so unfair
He took away my innocence
He forced me into silence
They say I should forgive
But he's made my life hard to live
I see him in my dreams
I hope he can hear my screams
It isn't fair that he's free
He ruined my life the day he touched me
I try to move forward
But it's as if I'm anchored
I'm trying real hard
But still I'm so scarred
I try to hide my pain
Even though it drives me insane
To you I may seem happy
But deep inside I'm really angry

Because behind my smile lie my fears
Because behind those laughs I hide my tears
I'm the one you call fake
Some days I just wish people knew how much I ache.

That girl....

A letter to that girl
That girl who sat by herself
That girl who doubted herself
That girl who was bullied
She was let down
A letter to that girl
That girl who was used
That girl who was manipulated
That girl who was gaslighted
She was left in pieces
A letter to that girl:
You are beautiful

You are wonderful
You are you
Don't let anyone take that away from you
And I know this world can knock you so far down
Trust me, I do
But it's all about picking yourself back up
Fighting back
And showing just who you are
Look at you, so strong
You showed everyone who you are
And even in the darkest moments
You pulled through
And you became you
So this is a letter to that girl
That girl who was knocked down
But she learned to get up
Everything is easier said than done
But I know how it all feels
For this is a letter to that girl
And that girl is me!

The one thing I should have said

He is a friend to remember,
A friend I miss too much.
I think about all the laughter
And even the times when our hearts touched.
I know you know the score now
As you look down from above.
You see me full of sorrow
'Cause so much of you I love.
I wish I had the chance,
But you decided you had to go.
That night you asked me for that answer,
I should have told you so.
But as every day has passed,
I can almost feel you near.
I just always thought you'd forever last
But now it's you I cannot hear.
Just one thing I should have said
While you were still down here,
But you stepped inside that bloody shed,
Though I will always hold you near.
I know to heaven you have been led.
You're the angel up above,
But just one thing I should have said.
It was you how much I LOVED.

Starbucks

At Starbucks, the world slows down
As the scent of freshly ground coffee fills the air
Baristas dance behind the counter
Crafting intricate lattes and cappuccinos with
care
The soft hum of conversation
Mixes with the gentle whir of espresso machines
A symphony of voices and laughter
Creating a comforting backdrop, serene
Sipping on a steaming cup of comfort
I find solace in the midst of chaos
A moment of respite, a pause in time
In this bustling haven, I am never at loss
With each sip, I am transported
To a place of warmth and familiarity
Starbucks, a sanctuary for the soul
A place where I find peace and clarity.

Memories

Memories are life's special moments
Borrowed from the passing of time.
Ghosts and shadows from bygone days,
Etched and stored inside our minds.
Our minds are a memory album
Where the past and present meet,
Memories we lovingly cling to
That make the heart skip a beat.
Some we would like to forget.
Some we love to treasure.
Some memories become precious gifts
That live on forever and ever.
Yes, memories are precious moments,
And I have quite a few,
The memories I treasure the most
Are those I made with you.

To make a mark on Earth

To learn while still a child
What this life is meant to be.
To know it goes beyond myself,
It's so much more than me.
To overcome the tragedies,
To survive the hardest times.
To face those moments filled with pain,
And still manage to be kind.
To fight for those who can't themselves,
To always share my light.
With those who wander in the dark,
To love with all my might.
To still stand up with courage,
Though standing on my own.
To still get up and face each day,
Even when I feel alone.
To try to understand the ones

That no one cares to know.
And make them feel some value
When the world has let them go.
To be an anchor, strong and true,
That person loyal to the end.
To be a constant source of hope
To my family and my friends.
To live a life of decency,
To share my heart and soul.
To always say I'm sorry
When I've harmed both friend and foe.
To be proud of whom I've tried to be,
And this life I chose to live.
To make the most of every day
By giving all I have to give.
To me that's what this life should be,
To me that's what it's for.
To take what God has given me
And make it so much more
To live a life that matters,
To be someone of great worth.
To love and be loved in return
And make my mark on Earth.

Mom, you are the reflection of WOW

MOM, you are the reflection of WOW.
You change sadness into happiness.
You change hate into love.
You change anger into smiles.
MOM, you are the reflection of WOW.
You are a nurse and a cook.
You are a teacher and a housekeeper.
You are an organizer and a planner.
MOM, you are the reflection of WOW.
You join broken hearts and motivate them.
You change every tear into a smile.
You are the brightest star in my darkest nights.
MOM, you are the reflection of WOW.
You love unconditionally.

You care deeply.
You inspire terrifically.
You encourage superbly.
You motivate enthusiastically.
MOM, you are the reflection of WOW.
You are a Wonder Woman
There is no person stronger, wiser, or more dedicated,
Than a mother.
MOM, you are the reflection of WOW.

Just wait for the sun

When everything's darkness
And you feel so alone,
When the rain doesn't stop
And you can't make it home,
When it feels like all is lost
And you just want to run,
It can't rain forever.
Just wait for the sun.
When family is pain,
When friends can't be found,
When you just want to scream
But you can't find the sound,
When it's not all your fault,
But you feel like you're done,
Just wait for the sun.
The sunshine will come.
The storm always passes.
It won't last forever.
The rain always stops and gives way to good weather.

The brightest and warmest of days still to come.
Please wait for the sun.
The sunshine will come.
People who need you,
People who still love you
Can warm up your soul like the sunshine above
you.
You're never alone,
No matter what's done.
Wait for the sun.
Just wait for the sun.
Dark clouds always pass.
I promise you a ton.
We're all waiting with you.
Just wait for the sun.

My daughter's wedding day

Soon is my daughter's wedding day.
And a wonderful thing it is
To see her so excited,
So happy to be his.
But once she was my baby girl,
My first born, the love of my life.
But now she is a woman
And to become his wife.
Once she was my baby girl,
Loved her daddy and her toys;
But then, I couldn't stop it,
She grew up and loved the boys.
From golden locks and lollipops,
She grew up straight and tall.
From baby things to a wedding ring;
How I loved her through it all.

I wish them both the best of luck;
With a prayer that my eyes will see
With tremendous love and happiness
And a fun-filled life to be!

To live behind a mask

My smile hides my tears.
My laugh hides my screams.
It's been this way for years.
Things aren't as they seem.
I always seem so happy.
With not a care in the world.
But you should know, sadly
Many things go untold.
Nobody really knows me.
They only know my cover.
But I wish I could let it free.
Let them know what's under.
But instead, I practice
My smiles in the mirror.
Then the next thing I do is
Make my fake laugh clearer.
What is wrong? You need help?
Is all they will ask.
So I have decided
To live behind a mask.

Living in the moment

Let me live in the moment.
Let me feel all that I can.
Let me cherish life for all it's worth,
With everything I am.
Let me see what's right in front of me,
With vision crystal clear.
And face what's waiting there for me,
With no hesitance or fear.
May I wake each day with gratitude,
For all my life may be.
And always feel that wonderment
At the world surrounding me.
May I welcome any strangers
With an open heart and mind.
And always stand for what is right
With all the strength that I can find.
Let me forgive myself for my mistakes,
While forgiving others theirs.
And never grow indifferent
But always strive to care.
Let me not forget what matters
In the scheme of every day,
To live each precious moment
In a kind and loving way.
For this moment now is everything,
Nothing matters but today.

So I'll willingly embrace it
And not let it slip away.
For it passes all so quickly,
And one chance is all we get.
And a life of wasted moments
Is a life filled with regrets.

In your eyes

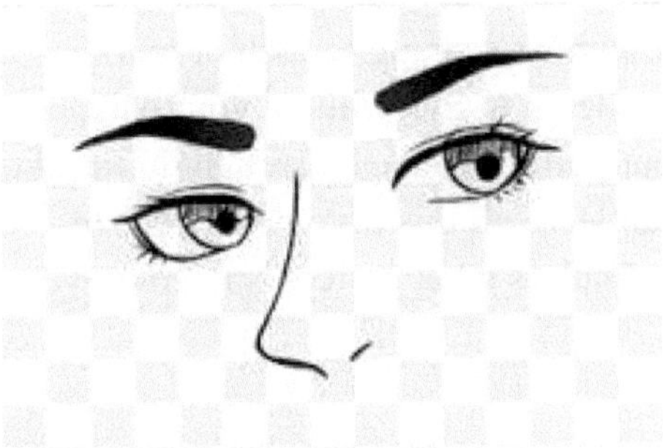

My heart flows through this icy land.
Come and take my lonely hand.
Show me how to make things right.
Cry these tears no more tonight.
Sing this sorrowful song into the air.
Try to live without a care.
Look up at the stars in the sky.
Dry those tears from your eye.
Lift your head, bring your smiles back.
Paint your world with color instead of black.
Undo your lies, make them true.
Don't let your anger take over you.
Open your eyes, what do you see?
There's so many things that you could be
If instead of thinking, you actually tried
And forgot about the tears you cried.
You could be living in a world of hope
And letting go, learning how to cope.
With everything life throws your way

And living your fullest every day.
You can force the shadows back to the dark.
Leave without a single scratch or mark.
You can learn to live without your pain,
Without putting yourself through this strain.
You can learn all this if you only realize
It only matters what perfect is in your eyes.

Something to base my life upon

I'm trying to find something to base my life
upon,
Something in this strange world that goes on and
on.
As the years go by and time fades away,
What used to be "good days" are now filled with
dismay.
Tomorrow comes, and then again it goes,
And my ambition to become something more
grows and grows.
Around the corner, yet miles away,
The life I want now gets closer each day.
All I've ever wanted was something to live for.
I don't want to be this little person anymore.
I've been basing my life upon what others think.
I wish I could go back and redo everything,
every time an eye would blink.
I've fought to become who I am and what I want
to be.
I have to remind myself that one day I will be
free,
Free from the rules I followed as a child,
When everything was a game and life was so
mild.

Now times have changed and I realize nothing is fair,
And sometimes it seems like nobody even cares.
It's like no one pays attention to what I feel is best for me
And what I think about the way some things should be.
I understand now that I'm pretty much on my own,
And I know a lot of what I can do will never be known.
All the time I think about everything I can't say, what I have to keep within,
And by doing this, my thoughts only get more complicated and deepen.
Soon I hope to find out who I am and what I am meant to become.
I want to know where I'm going.
I don't need to be reminded of where I came from.

Mistakes

It's only through mistakes we make
We learn where we went wrong.
It's only when we're far from home
We realize where we belong.
It's only when we close our eyes
Our dreams seem clear and bright.
It's only in our darkest hours
We truly see the light.
It's only when we lose our way
We pray to the stars above.
It's only through times of grief
We learn the true meaning of love.
It's only when all hope seems lost
And our weary journey seems so far,
When all the world's against you,
We learn how strong we really are.
All things are sent to try us.
We must strive and give our best.
I believe God is watching over us,
And he guides us in our quest.

An Angel like You

An Angel like you is hard to find,
One that touches you deep inside.
You've given me strength to carry on,
You've offered your hand to hold on.
When times are tough, I know you're there
to offer support and show you care.
If not for you, I would have drowned,
but you help keep me on solid ground.
I believe you were sent from the One above
because He knows the strength of your love.
You show that love in so many ways.
It helps me get through my darkest of days.
So for that, I write this poem for you
and tell you from my heart (DIL SE), THANK
YOU!

Time to go

The years have passed by
In the blink of an eye,
Moments of sadness
And joy has flown by.
People I loved
Have come and gone,
But the world never stopped,
And we all carried on.
Life wasn't easy,
And the struggles were there,
Filled with times that it mattered,
Times I just didn't care.
I stood on my own,
And I still found my way,
Through some nights filled with tears,
And the dawn of new days.

And now with growing age,
It's become very clear;
Things I once found important
Were not why I was here.
And how many things
That I managed to buy
Were never what made me
Feel better inside.
And the worries and fears
That plagued me each day,
In the end of it all,
Would just fade away.
But how much I reached out
To others when needed,
Would be the true measure
Of how I succeeded.
And how much I shared
Of my soul and my heart
Would ultimately be
What set me apart.
And what's really important,
Is my opinion of me,
And whether or not
I'm the best I can be.
And how much more kindness
And love I can show
Before the Almighty tells me
It's my time to go.

Before I knew how to be me

Before I became strong, I knew what it was like
To be weak,
How difficult it is to love yourself,
To find the wholeness that you seek.
Before I knew the light,
I have had my fair share of darkness, too,
Where my world fell into hopelessness
And I didn't know how to get through.
For I have known the tears it takes,
The courage to stand up again,
When you are broken down and bruised
And you know nothing but the pain.
You forget to appreciate love,
If you haven't seen the hate,
Till you forget the meaning of smile and
laughter,
And your heart is left abated.
I have known the strength and courage
It requires to get it right,
To face the things that hold you down
And hold your head up and fight.
Before I was who I am now,
I was someone I didn't want to be.
I was lost, battered, and defeated,
Before I knew how to be me!

The woman I wish to be

The woman I wish to be
She's flawless in her step
And graceful in her actions
She's unafraid of her abilities
And understands all that she is capable of
The woman I wish to be
Doesn't let criticism step into her mind
She owns her life and looks it in the eyes
She sees no barricades in her way
But rather stepping stones to better days
The woman I wish to be
Never compromises her life for a man
And couldn't care less for those who disapprove
Of her living life the way she can
The woman I wish to be
Is influential with a heart of gold
And even when strife echoes around her

Her love never withers like the old
The woman I wish to be
Sees the beauty all around her
And touches the stars
With her very eyes
The woman I wish to be
Lives so truthfully
Each day she owns, and night she prays
She's the perfect silhouette of modesty
The woman I wish to be
Trusts herself and lets love in as it be
And when she consoles others
She creates assurance that proves her to be
trustworthy
The woman I wish to be
Somehow I just know
Is deep within me.

I am what I am

I am what I am - a unique soul,
Crafted by the hands of time,
Shaped by experiences, both bitter and sweet.
I am the sum of all my thoughts,
The culmination of every tear shed,
And every smile shared with the world.
I am not defined by societal norms,
Or by the expectations of others.
I am my own masterpiece,
Unapologetically imperfect,
Yet perfectly flawed in my own way.
I am the whisper of the wind,
The roar of the ocean,
And the warmth of the sun on a winter day.
I am the laughter that fills a room,
And the silence that speaks volumes.
I am the strength that lies within,
The resilience that keeps me going,
And the vulnerability that makes me human.
I am what I am - a work in progress,
Forever evolving,
Forever learning,
And forever grateful for the journey.
I am not afraid to be myself,
To embrace my quirks and imperfections,
For in them, I find my truest self.
I am what I am - and that is enough.

The road less traveled

On the road less traveled, I found my way
Away from the crowds, where no one would sway
I walked alone, with courage in my heart
Ready to embark on a brand new start
The path was rugged, full of twists and turns
But I pressed on, for there was much to learn
I stumbled and fell, but I picked myself up
Determined to reach the mountaintop
The road less traveled is not for the weak
It requires strength and the courage to seek
A life of adventure, a life of dreams
Where nothing is quite what it seems
I faced my fears and conquered my doubts
I found my voice and learned to shout
I danced in the rain and sang with the birds
I found solace in the quiet words

On the road less traveled, I found myself
In the silence of nature, in the books on the shelf
I discovered my purpose, my reason to be
And I knew that I was finally free
So if you ever find yourself at a crossroad
And the road less traveled calls to your soul
Have courage, my friend, and don't be afraid
For on that path, your true self will be displayed.

From the perspective of a child

From the eyes of a child, the world is vast and wild
Each day filled with wonder and magic, each moment a new discovery
The world is a playground, a place to explore and play
Every moment is an adventure, every day a new story to tell
In the eyes of a child, everything is possible
Dreams are big and ambitions high, nothing is out of reach
Imagination runs wild, creating worlds beyond the realm of reality
Every moment is filled with excitement, every day a new opportunity
From the heart of a child, love is pure and unconditional
Each hug is given without hesitation, each smile shared without reservation
The world is a place of kindness and compassion, where everyone is a friend
Every moment is filled with joy, every day a new chance to spread love

In the mind of a child, the future is bright and full of potential
Each day is a chance to learn and grow, to become the person they dream of being
The world is a place of endless possibilities, where dreams can come true
Every moment is filled with hope, every day a new chance to make a difference
From the perspective of a child, life is a beautiful adventure
Each day a gift to be treasured, each moment a blessing to be cherished
The world is a place of beauty and wonder, where every day brings new surprises
Every moment is a miracle, every day a new chance to embrace the magic of childhood.

Childhood

In the garden of innocence, where memories are born,
Childhood dances in the golden light of dawn.
A time of wonder, a time of pure delight,
When the world is a canvas, and every color is bright.
Running through fields, with laughter in the air,
Chasing butterflies, without a single care.
Climbing trees, feeling the freedom of the sky,
Imagination soaring, reaching new highs.
Crayons and coloring books, sprinkled with creativity,
Building forts and castles, in a world of possibility.

Carefree days filled with simple joys,
Playing hide and seek, with all the neighborhood boys.
Skinned knees and scraped elbows, kisses from Mom,
Ice cream cones and popsicles, the perfect summers, called upon.
Bedtime stories and lullabies, whispered in the night,
Dreaming of adventures, under the moon's soft light.
Childhood is a treasure, a time we hold dear,
A time of innocence, without any fear.
So let's cherish these moments, for they will swiftly pass,
Childhood memories, forever cherished, forever last.

Like Mother, Like Son

In the quiet of the morning light
Mother and son, a beautiful sight
Their bond unbreakable, strong as can be
Like intertwined branches of a steadfast tree
A mother's love, a son's devotion
Mirroring each other in pure emotion
She raised him with tender care
He learned from her, their hearts a pair
Her gentle guidance shaped his ways
In her reflection, he sees his days
Her wisdom flows like a gentle stream
Nurturing his hopes and dreams
Her laughter, a melody in his ears
Her comfort, erasing all his fears
A mother's touch, a son's solace
Together, they find their place
Like mother, like son, a shared essence
In their love, there is no pretense

Their bond transcends time and space
In each other, they find grace
So hand in hand, they walk through life
Mother and son, through joy and strife
Their love a rainbow, forever aglow
A bond that only they can know
Like mother, like son, intertwined as one
In this journey of life, together they run
Forever connected, heart to heart
A love that will never depart.

Travel without boundaries

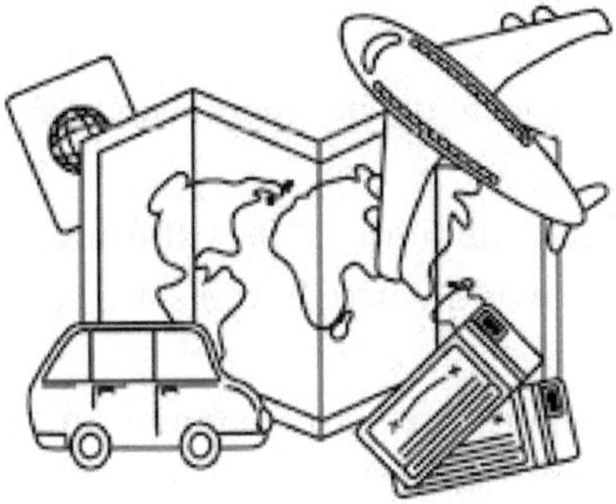

I dream of traveling without boundaries,
Of wandering through foreign lands,
Of seeing the world through open eyes,
And feeling the warm embrace of diverse
cultures.
I yearn to walk through bustling streets,
To taste exotic flavors on my tongue,
To breathe in the fragrant scents of faraway
places,
And to lose myself in the rhythm of unfamiliar
sounds.
I want to climb mountains that touch the sky,
To swim in oceans that stretch beyond the
horizon,
To dance under the stars in lands unknown,
And to feel the heartbeat of the world beneath
my feet.

I long to meet souls that speak a different
language,
To learn from those who see the world in a new
light,
To share stories with strangers who become
friends,
And to create memories that will forever ignite.
I imagine a world where borders are but lines on
a map,
Where passports are simply stamps on a page,
Where the only limits are those we place on
ourselves,
And where the journey is the destination, not the
stage.
So let me spread my wings and fly,
Let me roam free like a bird in the sky,
Let me follow the whispers of the wind,
And let me travel without boundaries,
unconfined.

Carpe diem

In a world where time slips through our fingers
Like grains of sand in an hourglass
We are urged to seize the day
To embrace the present moment
And live fully in the now
Carpe diem, they say
Seize the day and make it yours
For tomorrow is uncertain
And yesterday is but a memory
So we chase after the fleeting moments
Grasping at the intangible
Trying to hold on to the present
Before it fades away into the past
But can we truly hold onto time?
Can we capture the essence of the now?
Or are we simply running in circles
Chasing after shadows and echoes
Perhaps the secret lies not in seizing the day

But in surrendering to its flow
In embracing the uncertainty
And finding beauty in the impermanence
For life is but a series of fleeting moments
A dance of light and shadow
A symphony of joys and sorrows
And in the end, all we have are memories
So let us not waste our days in pursuit of the future
Or dwell in the shadows of the past
But let us live fully in the now
And cherish each moment as it comes
For in the end, it is not how many days we have lived
But how fully we have lived each day
That truly matters
So carpe diem, my friends
Seize the day and make it yours.

The quirky me

In a world of conformity, I stand out
With my quirks and eccentricities, I shout
I dance to my own rhythm, march to my own beat
I am unapologetically me, unique and complete
I wear mismatched socks and polka-dot shirts
I mix patterns and colors, creating wild works
My hair is a rainbow of hues, never the same
I embrace the chaos, reveling in the game
I speak in riddles and rhyme, my words a puzzle
I view the world through a kaleidoscope, a colorful juggle
I see beauty in the mundane, the extraordinary in the plain
I am the quirky me, unafraid to be different, unafraid to reign
I dance in the rain, sing with the birds

I find joy in the small things, words left unheard
I am not bound by society's rules, not confined by its chains
I am the quirky me, marching to my own refrain
So let me be odd, let me be strange
Let me be quirky, let me be deranged
For in my uniqueness, I find my strength
In my quirks, I find my truest self at length
I am the quirky me, a masterpiece of flaws
A kaleidoscope of wonder, a rebel with cause
I am unapologetically me, embracing my quirks
For in my eccentricity, I find my true worth.

Kaleidoscope

In a kaleidoscopic world, colors dance and swirl,
Shifting and changing in a mesmerizing twirl.
A tapestry of hues, a symphony of light,
Creating patterns that dazzle the sight.
Each turn reveals a new mosaic of beauty,
A never-ending display of artistic subtlety.
Shapes and forms blend in perfect harmony,
A visual feast for the eyes to see.
Like life itself, the kaleidoscope mirrors,
The endless cycle of beginnings and
disappearances.
A reminder that change is constant and
inevitable,
But also that beauty can be found in the
unpredictable.
So let us embrace the kaleidoscope of life,

Embracing the chaos and the strife.
For within the endless array of colors and shapes,
We find our own unique path to embrace.

When we believed in everything

Together we wrote our stories.
Together we sang our songs.
But now it's all gone.
Stashed away like photographs
inside my mind
in a place I have labeled "memories."
And sometimes,
when I flip through those pages,
thinking tenderly of the past,
remembering who we used to be-
sitting in class
having long conversations,
exchanging lyrics and words,
or just laughing 'til we couldn't breathe-
it fills me with a bitter-sweet ache,
and I just want to be little again.
Sometimes, random memories-
a reminiscent word said here,
a familiar melody heard there,
a burst of giggles and laughter-
catch me off-guard
and nostalgia floods my senses.
The desire to relive them,
to create once again

the everlasting from fleeting moments,
to feel the love that remains.
It grips me,
taking hold of my entire being.
My heart is throbbing again
with that sweet ache,
longing for what once was.
And that's when I realise,
it is but the wistful desire
of a child that never grew up
and learned just how to be.
So I had to settle for passing through the moments
like walking through doors,
only allowing my heart to flutter,
to flicker again with the bliss
I had once experienced.
It is a reminder
of a happiness I once owned,
of the love that remains,
of the things I no longer have...
and knowing that it will never come again
is what makes it so sweet.
A strange feeling fills my chest
as I leave this place.
As if I am not only going to miss
the people I love,
but also
the person I was at that time and place,

because I will never be that way again.
And I cling to it,
to that memory,
to that person I want to remain,
afraid to let it fade
to let it become a ghost,
a shadow.
Everything that I have loved
has become
everything I lost.
Wasn't it beautiful
when we believed in everything?

Starbucks- The Promise of a First Date

You had promised our first date at Starbucks,
Where the aroma of coffee lingered in the air,
We were going to sip on lattes and share stories,
In the cozy corner by the window with a view.
But time slipped away, like grains of sand,
And promises turned into forgotten dreams,
The stars witnessed our missed opportunity,
As we drifted apart in this vast universe.
The promise of a simple coffee date,
Became a symbol of what could have been,
A fleeting moment of connection lost,
In the bustling chaos of our lives.
Yet, in the silence of the night,
I still find myself yearning for that cup of coffee,
For the chance to sit across from you,
And see the world reflected in your eyes.
Our first date at Starbucks remains a memory,
A reminder of the paths we chose to take,

But in my heart, it lingers like a bittersweet melody,
A fleeting promise of what could have been.

The misunderstood

In every shadow, in every light,
Lies a story of the misunderstood,
A tale of pain, of loss, of fight,
Of dreams shattered, of hopes withstood.
They walk among us, unseen, unheard,
Their voices muted, their hearts aching,
Misjudged, labeled, their spirits stirred,
By the ignorance of those who keep mistaking.
The quiet ones, the introverts,
The ones who don't quite fit the mold,
They bear the weight of cruel asserts,
Yet carry on, with hearts of gold.
Their minds are vast, their thoughts deep,
Their souls aching to be understood,
But the world around them is too steep,
In prejudice and falsehood.
They don't seek pity, they don't seek fame,
Just a glimpse of understanding,
A touch of kindness, a shift in the game,
To see them for who they truly are, demanding.
So let us open our hearts, our minds,
To the ones who are often misunderstood,
For in them, a rare beauty we find,
A treasure full of stories, pure and good.
Let's listen to their silent cries,
And let their voices ring clear,

For in their truths, in their lies,
Lies a wisdom we all hold dear.

'Mom'ents- Happy Mother's Day

In the quiet 'Mom'ents of the morning
Before the hustle and bustle of the day begins
I sit and reflect on the woman who birthed me
The one who shaped me into who I am today
Her love is like a warm embrace
Soft and gentle, yet fiercely protective
She is my rock, my confidante, my biggest cheerleader
In her eyes, I see the reflection of my own worth
Her laughter is like music to my ears
Filling the room with joy and light
Her smile could light up the darkest of days
And her hugs are like a warm blanket on a cold night
She sacrificed so much for me
Putting my needs above her own
Her strength and resilience inspire me

To be the best version of myself
On this special day, I celebrate her
The woman who gave me life
A mother's love knows no bounds
It is endless, unconditional, and pure
So here's to all the moms out there
Who pour their hearts and souls into their children
You are appreciated, you are cherished
Happy Mother's Day, 'Mom'ents of love and light.

That stranger in the mirror

In the reflection staring back at me
Is a face that I just can't seem to see
It's a stranger, unfamiliar and unknown
A mystery that I'm left to decode alone
The eyes that gaze back are deep and wise
But hold secrets that they refuse to disguise
They tell a story of pain and sorrow
Of a past that's left a mark too hard to swallow
The smile that plays on those lips so tight
Tells of laughter that once shone bright
But now it's faded, lost in time
Replaced by a sadness that's too hard to climb
That stranger in the mirror, so silent and still
Holds a presence that's hard to fulfill
I reach out to touch the glassy frame

But all I feel is regret and shame
Who is this person that I see?
Is it really me, or just a fantasy?
I try to peel back the layers of disguise
But all I find are empty lies
That stranger in the mirror, so haunting and real
Reveals a truth that's hard to conceal
I must learn to embrace this unfamiliar face
And accept that I am my own saving grace.

That journey with a stranger

In the hustle and bustle of everyday life,
I found myself alone on a train,
Destined for a journey with a stranger,
A chance encounter that would leave a lasting stain.
As the train chugged along the tracks,
I couldn't help but steal glances at my companion,
A mysterious figure with a captivating aura,
Whose presence seemed to cast a spell upon.
We sat in silence for what felt like hours,
Both lost in our own thoughts and contemplations,
But there was something about the way he carried himself,
That sparked a curiosity and fascination.
With each passing mile, we exchanged knowing glances,

As if we were bound by an invisible thread,
And though we were strangers in the truest
sense,
There was a connection that couldn't be said.
As the sun dipped below the horizon,
And the sky was painted with shades of pink and
gold,
I found myself opening up to this stranger,
Sharing stories that I had never told.
And as the train came to a halt,
I realized that this journey with a stranger,
Had taught me more about myself,
Than any other encounter or danger.
For sometimes it takes a stranger's perspective,
To shine light on the parts of ourselves we hide,
And though our paths may never cross again,
I'll always treasure that journey with a stranger
by my side.

9 789360 942632

Printed by Libri Plureos GmbH in Hamburg,
Germany

Ich bin der Sturm

Gedichte aus dem Leben

Ines Wertenbroch

EINKLANG VERLAG

Zetel

Inhalt

Am Strand

Salzig wellt die Flut
in den Sand hinein.
Immer im gleichen Rhythmus,
als hätte das Land
das Meer gerufen.

Als sei der Strand
nur ein Teil
vom Grund des Wassers.
Einen Lebensraum bildend.

Meer und Strand
füreinander bestimmt.
Ein Bund aus den Gezeiten.

Ineinander verwoben
fließt das Wasser
in den feinen Sand.
Trägt der Grund das Meer.

Ein Versprechen
für die Ewigkeit

Ich bin der Sturm

Ich bin der Sturm,
der alle Perversion, Gelübde und Dogmen
wegpustet
wie eine Blüte.

Eine Seele in einem
menschlichen Körper.
Rein und aufgewacht.

Ich rede nicht.
Meine Waffe ist der Spiegel
in meinen Augen.
Mein Auftrag ist das
Einschmelzen der alten Rüstungen.

Ich bin einfach da.
Ich bin der Sturm.

Um die Welt
sanft in den Fluss zu bringen.
Die Frauen wieder zu ehren.
Die Männer fühlen zu lassen.
Alles an seinen Platz zu bringen.

Mit der Zartheit des Seins
jeden Krieg in Liebe aufzugeben.

Ich bin der Sturm.
Eine Seele in einem
menschlichen Körper.
Rein und aufgewacht.

Der Sturm,
der dich umarmt.

Glück

Gedankenlos,
tatenlos.

Kein Geben,
kein Nehmen.

Nur eine Melodie im Kopf,
so vor sich hin.

Liebe ist mein Seins-Zustand.

Wie eine Rosenknospe
am Abend vor ihrem Aufgehen.

Als Teil des Universums.

Bin ich.

Stillstand (Die alte Seele)

Die Zeiger der Uhr
drehen unaufhaltsam ihre Runden.

Das Rondell aus Zeit
wächst mit jeder Minute.

In der Mitte steht die alte Seele
für dich
im Stillstand
zwischen den Welten.

Der Kopf ist die Zeit,
das Herz der Kreis.
Am Körper ranken die Stunden.

Wie an einem alten Baum,
durch den du dein Zuhause findest,
wenn das Heimweh kommt.

Tanz der sieben Schleier

Ich drehe mich im Kreis,
trage sieben Schleier.

Leben ist Bewegung.

Der erste Schleier verhüllt meinen Kopf.
Keiner darf sehen,
was ich denke.
Ich wickle ihn herunter.

Der Blaue versteckt meine Augen.
Keiner darf sehen,
was ich sehe und wer ich bin.
Er schwebt zu Boden.

Tanzen ist Fließen.

Der Hellblaue vermummt meinen Mund,
weil ich nicht alles sagen kann.
Ich öffne den Knoten.

Der Grüne verbirgt mein Herz.
Ich darf nicht alles fühlen.
Ich löse ihn sachte auf.

Tanzen ist, im Moment bleiben.

Der Gelbe bedeckt meinen Bauch.
Keiner darf meine Gefühle sehen.
Er sinkt zu Boden.

Im Tanzen sich seiner selbst bewusst werden.

Der Orange umschreibt verschämt,
dass ich eine Frau bin.
Ich tanze ihn vom Körper.

Der Rote versteckt meine Wurzeln,
keiner darf sehen, woher ich komme.
Ich nehme ihn und werfe ihn zu den anderen.

Leben ist Entwicklung.
Jetzt stehe ich da
und tanze einfach weiter.

Tanzen ist frei sein.

Wir sehen uns wieder

Manchmal spüre ich
deine Anwesenheit.
Ein Fühlen,
kein Denken.

Ich wusste um dein Gehen.
Das ist der Preis,
erst einmal dafür.
Ohne dich zu sein.

Dein Geist ist hier.
Ich bin bei dir.
Ich lieb dich,
ja dich.
Du bist anders
schön.

Voller Freude
warte ich nicht.
Lebe jetzt.
Erwarte mich.

Wir werden uns
wieder sehen.

Liebesgefährten

Man lässt los
und lässt zu.

Ist nicht enttäuscht,
weil man nicht erwartet.

Gleich stark,
mit anderen Stärken.

Sie kämpfen nicht,
lassen sich einfach sein.
Sind nicht verstrickt,
nur verbunden.

Sie brauchen sich nicht,
sie lieben sich.

In Freiheit.

Hexentanz

Komm, liebe Schwester!
Verlass den Raum,
verlass dein Karma.
Es muss nicht dein Schicksal sein.
Du bist nicht deine Ahnin selbst.
Wache auf!

Komm liebe Schwester!
Du schläfst.
Ich möchte dich zum Tanzen bringen.
Du gehörst dir!
Gehorche nur
der Liebe zu dir selbst.

Komm, liebe Schwester!
Unser Sog ist das Leben selbst.
Unsere Geschichte zeigt nicht,
wer wir sind,

sondern nur die Menschen,
die sich vor dem Leben fürchten.
Wir wollten immer nur heilen.

Komm, liebe Schwester!
Ich lade dich ein,
deinem Mann eine ganze Frau zu werden
und den Kindern
eine ganze Mutter.
Heute dürfen wir alles sein.
Wache auf!

Komm, liebe Schwester!
Ich möchte dich
zum Tanzen bringen.

Novemberausflug

Ich gehe durch das Laub.
Der Wind fegt es
wirbelnd von den Wegen.
Darunter sehe ich ein Seil
und betrete es.

Ich atme.
Es schwankt,
doch es zieht mich höher,
Ich pendle mich ein,
Schritt für Schritt,
fest im Wind.
Arme aus Baumzweigen
greifen nach mir.
Aber ich gehe weiter.

Dann endet der Weg:

Spring!

Ich werde zur Taube
und fliege
mit dem Fluss des Windes.

Er streift mein Gefieder
und lässt mich
mich fühlen.
Ich atme.
Durch den Sturm.

Setze mich auf den Baum,
der nach mir greifen wollte.
Und schaue mir an,
warum es stürmt.

Irgendwann
möchte ich zurück.
Ich setze meine Füße
auf das Seil.
Werde von der Taube
wieder zu einem Menschen,
der Schritt für Schritt
auf dem Seil herunterbalanciert.
Zurückkommt.

Ich gehe wieder durch das Laub.
Und atme
den Sturm von unten
in meine Lunge.

Der Krieg ist vorbei

Die Erinnerungen
an meine alten Leben,
ich muss sie noch einmal fühlen.
In deine Augen sehen,
die Welt um mich sehen.
Den Schmerz,
vertrieben worden zu sein.
Kinder zu verlieren.
Zu wissen,
meine Kinder haben um mich geweint.

Der Krieg ist vorbei,
wenn wir uns entscheiden,
aus dem Alten herauszutreten.
Es funktioniert nicht mehr.

Sich nicht vom Sog
des Zerstörers ziehen lassen.

Dann umarmt dich die Liebe
wie ein kleines Kind.
Glaube ihr,
dass du geliebt wirst.

Trauere,
dass du dich
ihr nicht ergeben konntest.

Der Krieg ist vorbei,
wenn wir wieder
von der Liebe
geführt sind.
Wenn die Liebe
dem Krieg zeigt,
dass er nicht mehr gebraucht wird.
Die Grenzen sich lösen
und wir ohne Angst
wieder eins werden.

Ein Feiertag.

An mein Kind

Ich bin deine Mutter
und du bist mein Kind.
Ich möchte,
dass du glücklich bist,
du kleines Wesen.

Lass uns nicht kämpfen.
Ich bin auch ein Kind
in einem großen Körper,

Ich kenne deine Sorgen,
weil ich sie auch habe.
Und du spürst meine Gedanken.

Ich möchte dir soviel sagen.

Du hast Recht,
alles wörtlich zu verstehen,
weil du im Moment lebst
und deine Momente sind groß.
Worte lassen sich nicht zurückholen.

Lass uns nicht kämpfen.
Keiner hat Schuld.
Wir Großen bringen oft zuviel mit,
das dann zwischen uns steht.
Kämpfe nicht meine Kriege.

Wie leicht
kannst du noch
„Ich liebe dich" sagen.

Lass uns nicht kämpfen.
Ich weiß, dass du mehr weißt.
Ich würde nur verlieren.

Ich bin deine Mutter,
und du bist mein Kind.
Ich möchte nur,
dass du glücklich wirst,
du liebes kleines Wesen.

Tango

Leicht
mit einem Flügelschlag beginnt es.
Vertrauensvoll
geführt
durch den anderen.
Geleitet mit dem Lied.
Frei im Inneren.

Ein Funke in den Bewegungen.
Achtung voreinander.

Und die Liebe beginnt
mit einer Verbeugung.

Inspiration

Ich schenke
der Inspiration
mein Leben.

Ich habe sie
in meinen Körper eingeatmet
und lasse sie
als Worte,
als Bilder,
als Träume,
in allem, was ich tue
sich ausdrücken.

Mein Geist
ist der Atem.
Der Grund meines Daseins.

Der Atem,
der mich sein lässt.

Um so mehr ich inspiriert bin,
um so tiefer kann ich atmen,
um so mehr liebe ich,
um so mehr lebe ich.

Spuren

Der Mensch hinterlässt
immer eine Spur,
ob er lacht oder weint,
ob er da ist oder fehlt,
ob er glaubt oder lügt.

Mal achtsam, mal unbedacht
werden wir alle geprägt.

Spuren können Krater bilden,
Spuren können heilen.

Das Leben mit allem,
um uns herum
zwingt uns,
eine Gravur auf dieser Erde
zu schreiben.
Wir bleiben im Gedächtnis.

Spuren können heilen,
wenn sie aufgefüllt werden
mit dem Abdruck der anderen Seite:
aus Schmerz wird Freiheit,
aus Trauer wird Dankbarkeit,
aus Wut wird Frieden.
Und in all dem
wohnt die Liebe.

Ich gehe meinen Weg,
habe immer die Wahl.

Spuren können Krater bilden,
Spuren können heilen.

Aber wir
bleiben im Gedächtnis,
wenn wir Spuren
aus Liebe ziehen.

Der Baum (Weihnacht)

Es zieht mich
in den nahen Wald.

Der Boden ist weich
und voller Blätter.
Ich bleibe
vor einem der Bäume stehen.

Werden, Leben und Vergehen
zeigt er in seinem Dasein.
Seine Wurzeln,
sein Stamm,
seine winterkahlen Äste.
Er sammelt Kraft
für das neue Jahr.

Du bist wie ich,
scheint der Baum mir zu sagen.
Schlage deine Wurzeln
bis in das pulsierende Innere.

Lass ihre Wärme hochfahren
bis in deinen Kopf.
Von dort wachsen dir Äste.
Nimm mit ihnen das Licht auf.
Dann wirst du wachsen.

Eine funkelnde Kraft
läuft durch meinen Körper.
Als ich in die Krone schaue,
sieht es aus,
als leuchte es aus jedem Ast heraus.

Ich bin wie du.

Die Magie dieser Nacht
verbindet alles Lebendige
in einen wahren Frieden.

Heiligabend.

Dein Platz (im Leben)

Manchmal kommt es mir vor,
als wäre das Leben
eine Geschichte:
schon geschrieben,
aber noch nicht passiert.

Räume,
die es gibt,
ohne, dass man sie kennt.
Und doch
war ich irgendwann schon dort.

Wohin führt mich mein Weg?
Ob mein inneres Wissen
mich in die richtige Richtung zieht?

Hör auf zu denken,
dass du dich dabei verletzt,
sagt es.
Du kennst die Räume.
Du musst nur dort hingehen
und sie einrichten.

Nimm dich an die Hand,
lass dich leiten
und finde die Geborgenheit
mir dir.
Setze dich an dein Feuer.
Alles ist bereit,
wenn du es möchtest.

Alles ist schon geschrieben,
aber noch nicht passiert.

Wahre Liebe (Seelenhochzeit)

Wir haben uns versprochen,
uns an uns zu erinnern.

Geduldig lösen wir gegenseitig
uralte Krusten
Schicht für Schicht
von unseren Fassaden.
Zementierte Selbstzweifel,
Mutlosigkeit und Trauer.
Dicke Mäntel,
die uns voneinander fernhalten.

Wunden werden sichtbar.
Vergeben wir uns,
dass wir sie zum Heilen öffnen
wie ein Operateur mit seinem Skalpell.
Wenn der Schmerz uns immer wieder
bis ans andere Ende treibt.

Hinter all dem
weiß ich doch immer,
dass ich dich liebe.
Ohne Zeit und Raum.

Wir bergen allmählich
unsere Schätze aus den Mauern.
Ein Rad greift ins andere.
Bis wir den Sprung schaffen:
nach Hause kommen.
Endlich selbst daran glauben,
gut genug dafür zu sein.
Füreinander zu sein.

Wir haben uns versprochen,
uns an uns zu erinnern.
Frei und doch eins zu werden.
Jetzt stehen wir hier.

Der größte Dienst
an dein und mein Herz.

Das Herz-Universum

Das Herz
liegt in der Mitte
einer kleinen Muschel.
Sie steht einen Spalt weit auf,
damit es fühlen kann,
was um es herum passiert.

Wenn es unruhig wird
oder sich bedroht fühlt,
schließt es seine Schalen.

Es gibt nur ganz wenige,
die einen Schlüssel
für das Herz
in seinem kleinen Raum haben.

Davon träumt das Herz
und füllt sich auf,
wenn es sich an wunderschönen Tagen
einmal befreien kann.
Wenn ein anderes Herz da ist
und auf seinen Schlag antwortet.

Es wird stärker mit der Zeit
und schließt seine Muschel
nur noch selten.
Es ist auf die Welt gekommen,
um reicher und mutiger zu werden,
eingebettet in sein kleines
Herz-Universum.

Das durch das Leben erwachte Herz
liegt in der Mitte
seiner inzwischen großen Muschel.
Irgendwann hat es alle
seine Schläge getan.
Und geht.

Zurück bleiben zwei Schalen,
ausgekleidet mit Schichten
aus feinstem Licht.
Ein friedlicher Raum.
In der Mitte
der Abdruck unseres Herzens.

Die Trümmerfrau

In mir lebt noch die Trümmerfrau,
die baut und baut,
eisern noch für alles sorgt.
Die weint und weint,
weil der Mann ihr fehlt.

Die starke Trümmerfrau,
deren Füße auf Bröckeln stehn.
Den Kindern Vater und Mutter ist.
Getrieben von Sorgen,
was jeder Tag wohl mit sich bringt.

Die kleine starke Trümmerfrau,
die sich nichts zu wünschen traut.
Die Trümmerfrauen hinter sich hat.
Frauen, die auch Männer sind.

In einem Moment spricht sie zu mir:

Ich bringe dich aus der Ordnung.
Du bist doch keine Trümmerfrau!
Geh an deinen Platz.
Bitte lass mich schlafen geh'n.
Sei eine Frau,
die nicht auch Mann sein muss.
Hör auf zu bau'n.
Sei wieder Liebe.
Sei du selbst dir Existenz.

Die kleine Trümmerfrau verschwindet.
Mit ihr die Wut,
alles allein schaffen zu müssen.

Meine Trümmerfrauen:
Mutter, Großmutter, Urgroßmutter...

Ich nehm euch in den Arm.

Im Fluss

Weißt du, wohin du gehst?
Wenn du gehst.

Wie ein Stein in einem Fluss
treibt dich das klare Wasser.
Mal strömend, mal sachte
gleitest du über andere Steine.
Sie schleifen an dir
im Vorüberziehen.
Oben wird unten,
unten wird oben.
Wo könntest du in einem Jahr sein?

Das Wasser lenkt dich an ein Ufer
und du legst dich ins Gras,
um nachzudenken.
Wie wichtig ist ein kleiner Stein?

Verändert lässt du dich
wieder in das Flussbett ziehen.

Du fließt nicht mit
und bleibst immer öfter am Rand.

Weißt du, wohin du gehst?
Wenn du gehst?

Die anderen lassen sich treiben.
Nur du fühlst dich so schwer.

Ein Pärchen bleibt an deinem Platz stehen.
Sie nimmt dich in ihre Hand
als Kleinod für diesen Moment.
Sie glaubt, dass er irgendwann
wieder zu ihr findet.
Mir dir in der Hand,
gefüllt mit diesem Moment.

Weißt du, wohin du gehst?
Vertrau.
Wenn du gehst.
In den Fluss des Lebens.

Seelenhochzeit (11)

Wer bin ich wirklich?
Wenn viele alte Wunden geheilt sind.
Wenn gewohnte Schmerzen
sich aufgelöst haben.

Möchte ich wirklich so frei sein?

Ich danke all meinen Helfern,
die mich bis hier getrieben haben,
aus tiefstem Herzen.
Oft ohne es zu wissen,
mir den Spiegel vorhielten.
Nun löse ich mich heraus:

Heute verspreche ich mir,
nach langem Überlegen und ohne Furcht,
mich zu lieben und zu ehren
bis ans Ende meines Lebens.
In guten wie in schweren Zeiten.
Ich werde mich diesem Leben hingeben,
weil Mutter und Vater
mit mir entschieden haben,
auf dieser Erde zu sein.

Ich werde nun eins mit mir,
um Heimat zu finden.
Ich habe es gewählt.

Jetzt stehe ich hier
wie eine Königin der Stäbe
im Dienste.
Mir meine Stimme gebend.

Ja, ich möchte so frei sein.

Die Vollmondin

Würde es dich nicht geben,
wären Tag und Nacht
ohne Melodie.
Ohne Wandel.

Auf deinem Weg um die Erde
bestimmst du über
das Ruhen und das Werden.
Dein mächtiger Zyklus
lenkt das Wasser
in deinem Rhythmus.

Du bist die Frau des Universums.
Dein Mann, die Sonne,
durchscheint deinen schönen Körper
und überlässt dir die Nacht.
Gemeinsam schafft ihr
das Leben auf dieser Erde.
Eure Anwesenheit erlaubt
das Nähren
und das Loslassen.

Ihr bedingt euch,
keiner ohne den anderen.
Eure Strahlen finden sich
in einer zärtlichen Berührung
auf der Erde
wie zwei liebevolle Hände.

Würde es dich nicht geben,
wären Tag und Nacht
ohne Melodie.

Ohne Wandel.
Das Leben ohne
dein Wachen,
ein Leben
ohne Erwachen.

Auferstehung (der Liebe)

Ich weiß, dass du mich erkennen wirst.
Es gibt eine vertraute Melodie.
Ein Ahnung.
Du bist immer in meinen Gedanken.

Die Ahnung wird zum Erbeben.
Nichts ist mehr wie vorher.
Du machst dich auf den Weg zu mir.
Die Vorfreue wird dich führen.

Wir werden uns erkennen.
Es ist nicht vergebens.

Dann nehmen wir unsere Hände
und erstehen auf
in einem Tanz
als wären wir eins.

Tanzen nach unserer Melodie.
Eins und doch viel mehr.

Weil wir mutig waren
und doch nicht anders konnten,
feiern wir das Leben
nach der Auferstehung.

Die Stille

In meiner Stille
segle ich durch mich hindurch.
Möchte nicht mehr denken.
Nur fühlen,
was sich zeigt,
wie es sich zeigt.

Ich sinke tiefer.
Tränen lösen sich.
Die alte Sehnsucht
nach mir selbst.
Erwartungen und Gebilde
ertrinken darin.

Ich brauche nicht mehr.

Ich bin nun die Stille.

Die Perspektive

Hält man einen Spiegel
vor einen anderen,
gibt es ein immer neues
Bild vom Bild.
Wie ein Echo
wird es leiser und kleiner.
Mehr und mehr überlagert
von der Umgebung.

Mensch und Mensch
stehen sich gegenüber.
Je nach dem,
wie der Spiegel gebogen ist,
wo er steht,
ob Licht hineinfällt oder nicht.
Das Bild gerät immer
in eine neue Form.

Jeder Spiegel
seine eigene Wahrheit.

Die Hingabe

Lade den glücklichen Zufall
zu dir ein.
Kontrolliere es nicht,
sonst kann es nicht zu dir finden,
was für dich gedacht ist.

Selbst die Liebe
fühlt sich anders,
wenn du sie nicht erwartest.
Sie zeigt dir den Schmerz
und die Einsamkeit,
und gibt beiden
einen Kuss auf die Stirn.
Alles darf sein.

Suche nicht.
Warte nicht.
Der Tod kommt sowieso
als Symptom für das Leben.
Nichts kannst du kontrollieren.
Sei so frei
und lade den glücklichen Zufall
zu dir ein.

Was ich dir sagen will.

Es ist Frühling.
Es ist Abend.
Ich sitze hier
und möchte dir soviel sagen.

Versuche,
dir etwas zu schreiben.
Mein Herz klopft.
Es ist gerührt,
wenn es dich fühlt.
Du erinnerst mich an mich.
Alles ist so kostbar,
so wach geworden
durch dich.
Die Augenblicke mir dir.

Ach, so etwas schreibt man nicht.
Ich denke es nur
und schicke es dir
über mein Herz.

Ich sitze hier
und kann nichts tun,
um meinen Verstand zu beruhigen.
Denn das,
was ich dir sagen will,
ist viel größer.

Was ich dir sagen will:
solange ich meine eigene Schönheit
nicht erkenne,
kann ich nicht
bei dir sein.

Freiheit

Ich bin frei
von Langeweile und Warten.

Gedanken und Fragen
lösen sich in Nichts auf
und werden damit
in ihrer Wichtigkeit beantwortet.

Nichts beschäftigt mich,
nichts zieht seine Kreise,
wie es das sonst tut.

Ich bin frei
und möchte dabei
nicht gestört werden.
Gebe mir keine Mühe,
möchte nichts beweisen.
Nur dasitzen
und da sein.

Als wäre ich kein Mensch,
sondern ein Moment
samtweicher Leere.

Sommerregen

Sommerregen fällt auf mein Haar,
meine Schultern und meine Arme.
Er nimmt in jedem seiner Tropfen
die Wärme des Tages mit.

Klar und funkelnd
legt sich der Regen
auf die Blüten.

Meine Füße fühlen
das inzwischen nasse Gras.

Ich lasse den Sommerregen
seine flüchtigen Erinnerungen
auf mich heruntergleiten.
Er nimmt auch etwas von mir mit
und lässt es in den Boden fließen.

Sommerregen fällt auf mich
als wäre ich eine der Blüten,
ein Grashalm oder ein Blatt.

Alles ist erfrischt.
Ich weiß,
es kommt eine schöne neue Zeit.

Die Gänseblümchen

Ein Sommertag geht zuende.
Die Gänseblümchen schließen
ihre kleinen Blüten,
sehen etwas struppig aus
von der Sonne.

Ich erinnere mich an Sommertage,
die nach zu süßem Waldmeistersirup schmeckten.
Mit der alten Erna,
die immer krank war und jammerte,
sich aber nicht helfen ließ.
Ständig hatte ich Schuldgefühle,
weil ich nicht mochte,
was sie für uns Kinder tat,
und sie es doch so gut meinte.

Oder mit Ulrich,
der beim Schnaps lamentierte.
Nichts war gut genug.
Ich konnte nie etwas Kluges sagen.

Dann musste ich ins Bett,
obwohl es noch hell war.
Ich konnte nicht schlafen,

weil Erna und Ulrich
in meinem Kopf klebten
wie zu süßer Waldmeistersirup.

Diese beiden Menschen gibt es nicht mehr.
Wie sie vor ihren Gläsern saßen
und unharmonisch waren
wie ein verstimmtes Klavier,
das in einer verlassenen Kneipe steht.

Die Gänseblümchen schließen ihre Blüten.
Das hätte ich damals auch tun sollen.
Diese unwirklichen Sommertage.

Die beiden Alten haben mir gezeigt,
dass alles einem Plan folgt,
wir unsere Plätze im Leben haben.
Mal kurz, mal für den Rest unserer Zeit.
Es ist immer richtig,
damit Schmerz und Einsamkeit
von uns erkannt werden,
als etwas, das nicht zu uns gehören muss.

Die Gänseblümchen.
Es gibt keins,
das perfekter wäre als ein anderes.

Die Schönheit

Die Schönheit
beginnt in der Tiefe.
Es gibt kein Ende,
denn wer bestimmt
die Schönheit?

Ein Licht,
das durch die Augen strahlt.

Es geht nicht darum,
glatt zu sein,
sondern überhaupt zu sein.
Ohne Status,
ohne Kleidung,
ohne Erwartung.
Sie hat keinen Preis.

Die Bewunderung,
die sie möchte,
ist nicht eitel
oder um Zuwendung zu bekommen.

Sie möchte geben.

Aus ihrer Tiefe heraus.

Ein Herz

bis an den Rand

mit Freude füllen.

Familie

Familie ist nicht allein,
was uns auferlegt wurde.
Es ist eine Aufgabe,
in der es Gaben und Schwere
über Generationen gibt,
um irgendwann
herausgehoben und angeschaut zu werden.
Würde dabei ein einzelner fehlen,
wäre es nicht das System,
das es ausmacht.

Familie ist ein Geschenk,
auch wenn es uns
oft nicht so scheint.
Sie ist eine große Kraft
aus Verbindung und Wachstum.

Familie ist eine Kraft,
die hinter alles Auferlegte
sehen kann.
Wo erst Frieden herrscht,
wenn die Verbindung,
die Liebe,
gelebt werden kann.

Mittsommernacht

Die Sonnenseite.
Die Leichtigkeit.
Die Fülle.
Wenn man genießt,
was im Moment sich zeigt.

Die Schattenseite
als Kontur für das Licht.
Denn ohne die Nacht,
würden wir den Tag nicht verstehen.

Doch einmal im Jahr
leuchtet selbst die Nacht.
Verbindet leichtfüßig
die Unterschiede
in einem Fest der Natur.

Der Liebe entgegen

Siehst du dich?
Die leise Musik
deiner Seele
führt dich.
Führt dich
zu dem,
was wirklich wichtig ist.

Fühlst du dich?
Die leise Stimme
deiner Seele
führt dich,
führt dich.

Eines Tages
ist es nicht nur Hoffnung
auf diese Freiheit.
Nicht mehr in die
kleinere Liebe.

Eines Tages,
voller Vertrauen
der großen Liebe entgegen.
Zu dir.

Bleib stehen!

Wir sind es nicht gewohnt,
auf unser Herz zu hören.
So wie wir müde sind
und dann schlafen gehen.

Was für ein Verrat an unsere Seele,
wenn wir uns nicht
der Liebe stellen.
Nicht nur zum Überleben hier sind.

Bleib stehen!
Lass los!
Spring in dein Herz!
Selbst, wenn du einmal
die Luft anhalten musst.
Spring in deinen Himmel
auf Erden.
Wenn du die Gelegenheit hast.

Wie unendlich

Das Leben ist uns nur geliehen.
Ein kurzer Moment,
der nicht hätte passieren dürfen.
Uns alles nimmt.
Uns alles gibt.

Später wird sich zeigen,
warum etwas geschehen ist.
Alles, was uns zweifeln und leiden lässt,
verändert uns für immer.

Sieht man das Leben
aus dem Blickwinkel der Ewigkeit,
gibt es nur
Wachstum und Erkenntnisse.

Das Leben ist uns nur geliehen.
Wir müssen gehen,
wir kommen wieder.

Umso mehr wir jetzt
von unserer Tiefe verstehen,
umso weniger wird nötig sein.

Ein Moment
kann uns alles nehmen.
Kann uns alles geben.

Die Ohnmacht zeigt uns,
wie endlich wir sind.
Das Vertrauen in alles Sein
wie unendlich.

Das Lied

Es gibt ein Lied,
das mich ruft.
Weil es mich begleitet.
Meine Kindheit hervorholt
und jede Sehnsucht,
die danach kam.

Wie ein Kinderlied
dreht es sich im Kreis,
mit einer einfachen Melodie.

Die ersten Takte
geben mir das Gefühl,
jemand ist da.
Und die Suche hört auf.

Es gibt dieses eine Lied,
das mich ruft.
Wie jemand,
der den Arm um mich legt.

Dieses Lied begleitet mich
und lässt mich
die eine Sehnsucht erkennen:
die zu mir.

Abschied (Ich bin der Sturm II)

In den letzten Tagen
bin ich unruhig gewesen.
Mein altes Leben kommt mir vor
wie eine Pappkulisse.
Als wäre alles bisher
nur eine Illusion gewesen,
die ich als Leben bezeichnet habe.
Ich kannte es nicht anders,
kaum einer kannte es anders.

Traurigkeit und Scham
überfallen mich,
weil ich so anders geworden bin.
Weil ich nicht bleiben kann.
Ich würde verhungern
und an nichts mehr Freude haben.

Vielleicht war ich
im tiefsten Innern
doch immer falsch hier.
Hab mich angepasst,
so gut es ging.

Vielleicht war ich die Lüge,
war immer der Sturm
mit unbändiger Kraft.
Ich hab mich selbst
vor mir gefürchtet.

Auch, wenn wir uns das Leben
schwer gemacht haben:
ich weine um euch,
werde euch und alles Vertraute vermissen.
Weil ich euch nicht zeigen kann,
wie schön mein Weg
für mich ist.

Ich wünsche mir,
dass wir uns am Ende wiedersehen.
Als die, die hinter
den Kulissen hervortreten.
Werdet auch zum Sturm,
der ihr wirklich seid.

Ein Schmetterlingsleben

Wie viele Schmetterlingsleben
passen in ein Menschenleben?

Wie irdische Engel,
so zart als könnte ein Regen
ihre Flügel zerstören,
sind sie zu einer bestimmten Zeit da.

Soviel Veränderung in einem Leben.
Keiner weiß,
wohin sie dann gehen.
Sie sind immer zu finden,
wo die Blumen sind.

Wie irdische Engel
können entpuppte Menschen sein.
Die still ihre Flügel ausbreiten.
Die sich die Schmetterlinge ansehen
und wissen,
wie schmerzhaft die Befreiung
vor dem ersten Flug ist.

Doch es lässt sie immer
dorthin gehen,
wo sie hingehören.

Nur ein Schmetterlingsleben
passt in ein Menschenleben.

Das ent-schlossene Herz

Hat sich ein Herz ent-schlossen
für die Liebe,
möchte es strömen,
ohne begrenzt zu werden.
Die gewohnte Furcht
zerspringt wie ein
altes sprödes Glas.

Das geöffnete Herz
kann sich begeistern
wie ein Kind.
Es bleibt stehen
und sieht anderen Herzen
bis auf den Grund.
Es kann nicht verletzt werden,
weil es nicht zu stolz ist,
um zu bitten.
Weil es nicht zu bescheiden ist,
um selbst zu erhören und zu segnen.

Es legt die Hand auf.
Es vertraut und sagt:
„Ich bin".

Wenn ein anderer das Herz
anhalten und beschützen will,
geht es auf den Schatten zu.
Es weiß, dass der sich nur
selbst wandeln kann.
Es spielt nicht Gott,
es lässt den Dingen
ihren sinnhaften Lauf.
Aber es ist zu spüren,
dass das Herz dort gewesen ist.

Das geöffnete Herz weiß,
dass Kämpfen,
Warten und Beschäftigtsein
den Strom in ihm begrenzen,
der seine wahre Lebenskraft ist.

Es legt die Hand auf.
Es vertraut und sagt:
„Ich bin".

Einfach nur: „Ich bin".

Nachtlied (der Trümmerfrau)

Der Tag ist vorbei.
Zeit, sich einen Schritt
zur Seite zu stellen,
um zu sehen,
was gewesen ist.

Uns wurde genommen,
um unsere Liebsten zu trauern.
Ihr seid nicht vergessen.

Es ist still.
Der Tag hat sich ausgelebt.
Die Nacht legt sich
mit ihrer Dunkelheit darüber.
Beschützt und einsam zugleich.

Uns wurde genommen,
um unsere Liebsten zu trauern.
Ihr seid nicht vergessen!

Auch wenn unser Tag vorbei,
wir sind nicht schuldig!
Wir geben nicht auf!

Es ist so still.
Einer der vielen Tage ausgelebt.
Ich weine heimlich,
solange ich es noch kann.

Du bist nicht vergessen.

Frieden in meinen Wurzeln

In Gedanken sehe ich
jeden einzelnen von euch
vor mir wie in einem Fotoalbum.
Jeder Kampf war nur
ein Ringen um Liebe und Gesehenwerden.
Ihr habt alle das getan,
was euch dafür richtig schien.

Ich dachte,
es wäre auch in meiner Welt richtig.
Dachte, ihr seid meine Welt.
Ich als Kind in dieser Familie.

Sich zu lösen ist schmerzhaft,
weil es bisher so vertraut war.
Weil ich glaubte,
es sind meine Wurzeln.
Eure Erwartungen an mich,
das wäre ich.
Aber ich bin es nicht,
kein Konstrukt eurer Gedanken.

Für den einen bin ich die Tochter,
für den anderen die kleine Schwester,
die große Schwester.

Sich zu lösen heißt,
erwachsen zu werden.
Die volle Verantwortung zu übernehmen.
Keiner hat Schuld,
alles war zu dem Zeitpunkt richtig.

Ich war ein Kind dieser Familie.
Eine gemeinsame Geschichte,
jeder aus seiner Perspektive.
Jeder eine andere Geschichte.
Jeder ein einzelner Mensch.

Kein Kampf mehr.
Es fügt sich nach vielen Jahren
mit den gleichen Menschen
eine neue Familie zusammen.
Ohne Bitterkeit und Erwartungen.
Mit Raum für mehr Liebe.

Frieden in meinen Wurzeln.

Der Tag dazwischen

Es ist noch nicht Herbst
und auch kein Sommer mehr.
Der Himmel ist trüb,
kein Wind weht.

Ich fühle mich
wie zwischen zwei Polen,
zu keinem dazugehörig.
Wie in einem Traum
möchte ich wegrennen
und kann es nicht.
Dabei gibt es keinen Grund,
sich zu beeilen.
Es ist noch nicht soweit.

Heute bin ich weich
und dankbar für das,
was ich erlebt habe.
Aber auch ratlos.
Es gibt solche Tage.
Der kühle Himmel
fegt durch meinen Kopf.
Ist es sinnlos,
darüber nachzudenken?

Ich bin müde
vom Rennen ohne weiterzukommen.
Es sind nur Gedanken.
Fäden verlieren sich wieder.
Weder Plus noch Minus.
Keine Anziehung.

Der Tag dazwischen
hat keine Antwort.
Anscheinend ist es noch nicht soweit.

Alles wird wieder gut

Ich habe dein Bild so oft angesehen,
dass es verblassen müsste.
Mit immer neuen Augen.
Du bist so schön.
Du bist so stark.
Du bist so kühl.
Du wirst mir fremd.

Wie ein Kind sitze ich da,
wie zersplittert,
wenn ich bei dir war.
Es hat mich nicht glücklich gemacht.
Hab mich von mir getrennt,
um bei dir sein zu können.

Wie in einem Sog
bin ich um dich gekreist.
Um dir zu gefallen.
Wie ein Kind um seine Mutter,
um seinen Vater,
wenn es sie gebraucht hat.

Mein Schmerz ist alt.
Vertraut.
Das war meine Liebe zu dir.

Es wird Zeit,
dass ich das Kind in mir
auf den Schoß nehme
und ihm sage:
„Alles wird wieder gut!“

Die Liebe einer Frau

Die Erde ist unser Spielplatz.
Trotzdem taumeln wir oft
wie Flaschen im Meer.
Wir wünschen uns
ein warmes Gefühl im Herzen.

Sein oder nur nicht zu sehen,
ist die Antwort auf den Sinn.

Früher war ich ergriffen
von all den Unmöglichkeiten.

Die Erde ist unser Spielplatz.
Ein Fest, bei dem sich
Räume und
immer andere Menschen öffnen,
wenn wir zu feiern bereit sind.

Fragst du dich,
was ich mache,
wenn ich allein bin?
Ob ich warte?
Ob ich mich einsam fühle?

Ich sitze hier,
mit der ganzen Liebe einer Frau.

Liebesgefährten (II)

Wir suchen uns mit dem Herzen aus.
Nicht aus Einsamkeit.
Nicht, um Schmerz zu verstecken.

Wir nehmen unsere Hände,
so zart,
als wäre es die Seele des anderen selbst.

Wir lassen uns unseren Frieden,
als wäre es unser eigener.

Unsere Herzen werden
mit jedem Wort größer.

Wir finden uns nur,
um ein Ort der Liebe zu sein.

Ines Wertenbroch

Die Diplomsozialpädagogin, Jg. 1981, wuchs mit drei Geschwistern in Emsbüren (Emsland) auf. Seit 2006 lebt sie in Jever (im Landkreis Friesland) und ist Mutter zweier Kinder. Ihre ersten Gedichte schrieb mit 13 Jahren. Bald darauf gab es kleine Veröffentlichungen im Osnabrücker Kirchenboten.
In ihrer Teenager-Zeit hat sie sich viel mit Lyrik befasst, und sie schrieb auch regelmäßig selbst Gedichte. Später kam verstärkt das Malen und das Schreiben von Kurzgeschichten hinzu.

Sie hat mit Kindern, Jugendlichen, psychisch Erkrankten und alten Menschen zusammengearbeitet. Ihr Beruf ist für sie gleichzeitig Berufung, denn sie beobachtet gern Lebenswege und begleitet - wenn möglich - entlastend und hilfreich.

Die Frage nach dem tieferen Sinn des Lebens ist zentraler Kristallisationspunkt ihres Denkens und Schreibens. Mit den Gedichten möchte sie das Leben mit seinen verschiedenen Seins- und Gefühlszuständen symbolisieren. Denn alles darf sein: Selbstliebe, Zustände von Leere, Einsamkeit, innere Veränderungen, Liebe zu einem anderen Menschen, zu den eigenen Kindern und der Natur, Fragen, Ängste, Trauer.

Sie selbst formuliert es so: „Wie nähern wir uns als Menschen unserem Lebenssinn? Wie fühlt sich Liebe an, die nicht braucht oder abhängig von etwas ist? Wie formen uns andere Menschen? Menschlich machen uns die Gefühle. Die Gedichte möchten anregen, aus dem Funktionieren herauszukommen und sich darauf zu besinnen, was ich als Mensch in dem mir gegebenen Leben erleben und erreichen möchte."